LIBERIA

...in Pictures

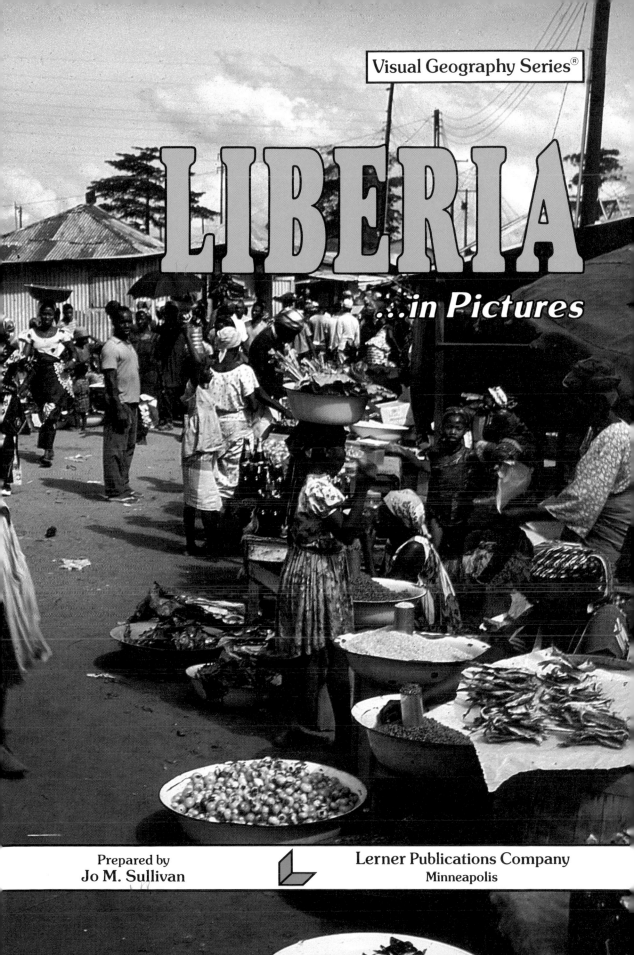

Visual Geography Series®

LIBERIA

...in Pictures

Prepared by
Jo M. Sullivan

Lerner Publications Company
Minneapolis

Courtesy of Agency for International Development

Surrounded by his family, a young Liberian shows his skill in playing the xylophone.

This is an all-new edition of the Visual Geography Series. Previous editions have been published by Sterling Publishing Company, New York City, and some of the original textual information has been retained. New photographs, maps, charts, captions, and updated information have been added. The text has been entirely reset in 10/12 Century Textbook.

LIBRARY OF CONGRESS CATALOGING-IN-PUBLICATION DATA

Sullivan, Jo Mary, 1946–
    Liberia in pictures / prepared by Jo M. Sullivan.
      p. cm.—(Visual geography series)
    Rev. ed. of: Liberia in pictures / by Camille Mirepoix.
    Includes index.
    Summary: Describes the land, climate, history, government, economy, culture, and people of the west African country settled by freed American slaves.
    ISBN 0–8225–1837–6 (lib. bdg.)
    1. Liberia. [1. Liberia.] I. Mirepoix, Camille. Liberia in pictures. II. Title. III. Series: Visual geography series (Minneapolis, Minn.)
DT624.L55 1988
966.6'2—dc19   87–26470

International Standard Book Number: 0–8225–1837–6
Library of Congress Card Catalog Number: 87–26470

VISUAL GEOGRAPHY SERIES®

Publisher
Harry Jonas Lerner
Associate Publisher
Nancy M. Campbell
Senior Editor
Mary M. Rodgers
Editor
Gretchen Bratvold
Illustrations Editor
Karen A. Sirvaitis
Consultants/Contributors
Jo M. Sullivan
Sandra K. Davis
Designer
Jim Simondet
Cartographer
Carol F. Barrett
Indexer
Sylvia Timian
Production Manager
Gary J. Hansen

Photo by Peter Schwab

A woman walks from her village to the nearest market.

Acknowledgments

Title page photo courtesy of John Dean, Eliot Elisofon Archives, National Museum of African Art, Smithsonian Institution.

Elevation contours adapted from *The Times Atlas of the World,* seventh comprehensive edition (New York: Times Books, 1985).

Manufactured in the United States of America
3 4 5 6 7 8 9 10 – JR – 03 02 01 00 99 98 97 96

Liberian farm workers check the growth of an experimental rice field near Monrovia, the capital of Liberia.

Contents

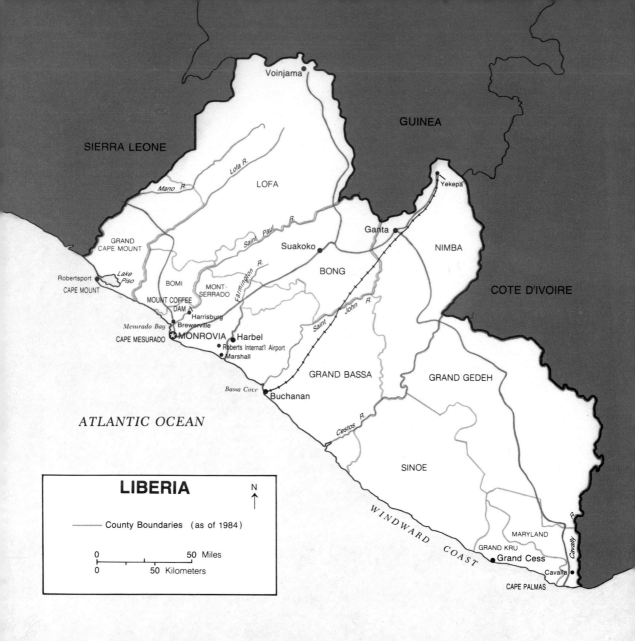

Voinjama

GUINEA

SIERRA LEONE

Lofa R.

Mano R.

LOFA

Yekepa

Saint Paul R.

Ganta

Suakoko

NIMBA

GRAND
CAPE MOUNT

BONG

COTE D'IVOIRE

Robertsport

*Lake
Piso*

BOMI

CAPE MOUNT

Farmington R.

MONT-
SERRADO

MOUNT COFFEE
DAM

Harrisburg

Saint John R.

Brewerville

Mesurado Bay

MONROVIA

Harbel

CAPE MESURADO

Roberts Internat'l Airport

Marshall

GRAND BASSA

GRAND GEDEH

Bassa Cove

Buchanan

ATLANTIC OCEAN

Cestos R.

SINOE

LIBERIA

N

— County Boundaries (as of 1984)

0   50 Miles

0   50 Kilometers

WINDWARD COAST

MARYLAND

GRAND KRU

Cavalla R.

Grand Cess

Cavalla

CAPE PALMAS

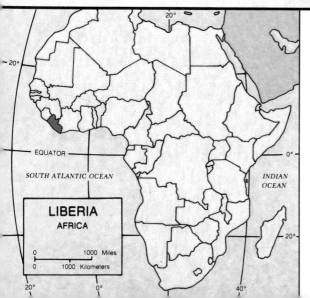

20°

20°

EQUATOR

SOUTH ATLANTIC OCEAN

INDIAN
OCEAN

0°

LIBERIA
AFRICA

0   1000 Miles

0   1000 Kilometers

20°

20°

0°

40°

METRIC CONVERSION CHART
To Find Approximate Equivalents

WHEN YOU KNOW:	MULTIPLY BY:	TO FIND:
AREA		
acres	0.41	hectares
square miles	2.59	square kilometers
CAPACITY		
gallons	3.79	liters
LENGTH		
feet	30.48	centimeters
yards	0.91	meters
miles	1.61	kilometers
MASS (weight)		
pounds	0.45	kilograms
tons	0.91	metric tons
VOLUME		
cubic yards	0.77	cubic meters
TEMPERATURE		
degrees Fahrenheit	0.56 (*after* subtracting 32)	degrees Celsius

The arrival of an airplane brings villagers rushing to the airstrip.

Introduction

With a culture created by many ethnic groups, Liberia is a diverse and sometimes divided African country. Liberia—derived from the Latin word for freedom—was founded in 1821 by free black settlers from the United States, whose ancestors had been taken from Africa as slaves. The newcomers chose a place in West Africa for their new home, an area next to Sierra Leone, where Great Britain had established a colony for former slaves in 1787.

African farmers, fishermen, and traders lived in the region where the U.S. blacks settled. The newcomers occupied the coastal strip that lay within the great forest belt of West Africa, an area with abundant rainfall. For over a century this English-speaking, Christian minority lived in uneasy isolation, at odds with local African groups and threatened by European colonial powers.

In the mid-nineteenth century, when regional African leaders and European traders challenged Liberia's authority, the United States stepped in with military assistance. Since then, U.S. influence has been primarily on the Liberian economy in the form of foreign aid and corporate investments. In addition, Liberia continues to be of strategic importance to the United

States. A U.S. naval tracking station is located near the capital city of Monrovia, as is Africa's only transmitter for Voice of America broadcasts.

A period of economic prosperity in the 1950s and 1960s was followed by a downturn in the 1970s, when world demand and prices for Liberia's rubber, iron ore, and cash crops dropped drastically. Liberia faced a declining economy, rising urbanization, and political strife.

Some of the recent political conflicts stem from the age-old tensions between the Americo-Liberians and the African Liberians. The Americo-Liberians are a minority population of U.S.-descended blacks, who ran the country beginning in the mid-nineteenth century. The Africans, on the other hand, make up the majority and are members of a variety of strong ethnic communities that have lived in the region for centuries. A military coup d'état in 1980 brought the first purely African administration into Liberian politics. In 1989 rebel armies successfully overthrew the new regime and plunged Liberia into a civil war. As the war continues, militias have split into more and more factions, often along ethnic lines. At any given time, as many as half a dozen military leaders have fought for control of Liberia. The ongoing conflict has all but destroyed the country's economy and is responsible for the death or displacement of hundreds of thousands of citizens.

If the war can be successfully ended, Liberia has the potential to be a prosperous nation. But as long as military warlords squabble over power, the country will remain in chaos.

Liberia's rubber products—some of which are being loaded on this barge at Harbel—brought economic prosperity until the 1970s, when the price of rubber dropped substantially.

Waves continually crash against the beach at Grand Cess in southeastern Liberia.

1) The Land

Nestled in the center of the West African coast, Liberia is one of the smaller countries on the African continent. The nation covers an area of 43,000 square miles, which is about the size of the state of Tennessee. Liberia's border runs for approximately 350 miles along the Atlantic Ocean and extends inland from the coast for roughly 150 miles. The nation shares boundaries with Sierra Leone on the west, Guinea on the north, and Côte d'Ivoire on the east.

Topography

Lying completely within the tropics, Liberia's territory is divided into three topographical regions. The first area is a 10- to 25-mile-wide strip of land along the Atlantic coast, which receives plenty of rain —sometimes as much as 200 inches annually. Fertile land and nearby harbors have encouraged settlement in this part of the country. Liberia's three largest cities— the capital city of Monrovia, the rubber production center of Harbel, and the port of Buchanan—have flourished among the lagoons and marshes that characterize the landscape. The low coastline—carved by small bays—is interrupted by three hills: Cape Mount, Cape Mesurado, and Cape Palmas.

The terrain rises gradually from the seacoast into the second region, where the landscape begins with rolling, grass-covered hills. A series of high plateaus

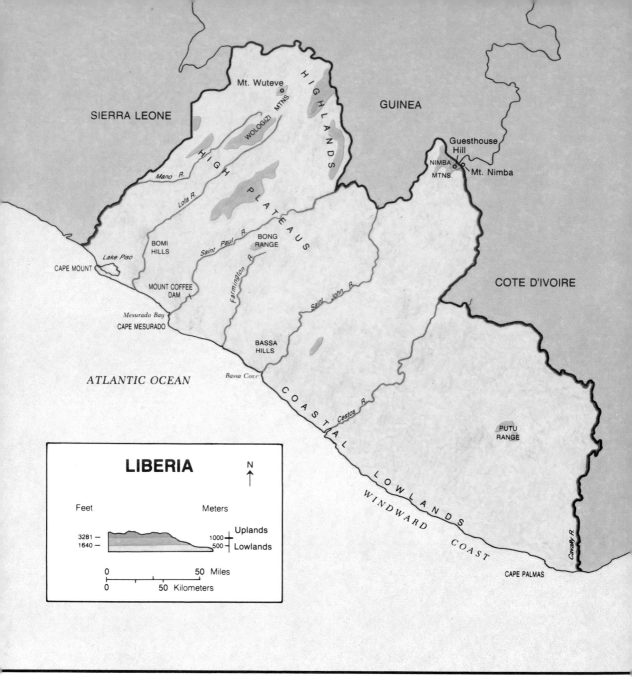

The map shows Liberia with the following labeled features:

SIERRA LEONE

GUINEA

Mt. Wuteve

HIGHLANDS

WOLOGIZI MTNS.

HIGH PLATEAUS

Mano R.

Lofa R.

Guesthouse Hill

NIMBA MTNS.

Mt. Nimba

COTE D'IVOIRE

BOMI HILLS

Saint Paul R.

BONG RANGE

Farmington R.

CAPE MOUNT

Lake Piso

MOUNT COFFEE DAM

Saint John R.

Mesurado Bay

CAPE MESURADO

BASSA HILLS

ATLANTIC OCEAN

Bassa Cove

COASTAL LOWLANDS

Cestos R.

PUTU RANGE

WINDWARD COAST

Cavally R.

CAPE PALMAS

LIBERIA

N

Feet   Meters

3281 —   1000 — Uplands
1640 —   500 — Lowlands

0   50 Miles
0   50 Kilometers

develops, interrupted by the Bomi Hills. The site of Liberia's first iron ore mine, these hills were important to the national economy in the 1960s and 1970s. In addition, dense undergrowth and thick stands of tropical rain-forest blanket the region.

Farther inland are the highlands, which generally exceed 3,000 feet above sea level. The Nimba Mountains, whose foothills begin in neighboring Côte d'Ivoire, stretch into the Republic of Guinea. Guesthouse Hill (4,613 feet)—Liberia's highest peak—lies within the Nimba range. To the west, the Wologizi Mountains are situated near Liberia's border with Sierra Leone. Mount Wuteve (4,528 feet) is the tallest peak in this chain and lies north of the Bong range, which is located between the Saint Paul and Saint John rivers in the Liberian interior.

Rivers, Lakes, and Lagoons

Liberia's rivers generally flow southward from the country's interior to the Atlantic Ocean. Beginning in the west, the Mano River forms part of Liberia's border with Sierra Leone. The Lofa River begins in the Wologizi Mountains and travels the width of Liberia to empty its waters into the Atlantic, east of Robertsport.

Perhaps the most important commercial river in Liberia is the Saint Paul, which flows for 125 miles, reaching the Atlantic just west of the dock facilities of Monrovia. Both the Saint John and Cestos rivers irrigate farmland in central parts of Liberia and deposit their waters at port cities. Following the country's eastern border with Côte d'Ivoire, the Cavally River begins in the Nimba Mountains and serves as one of the more important water routes in the region. Sandbars, rocks, and occasional rapids make navigation difficult along all of these rivers, but the water-

Photo by Sally Humphrey

Seasonal rains drench Liberia, causing crops that prefer a warm, wet climate to flourish.

Photo by Sally Humphrey

The Farmington River begins in central Liberia and flows through the rubber plantation at Harbel before emptying into the Atlantic Ocean at Marshall.

Located at Harrisburg, about 15 miles northeast of Monrovia, the Mount Coffee Dam provides hydro-electric power to the capital.

Liberia's tropical climate is ideal for growing trees. As a result, timber—here being processed at a Monrovia sawmill—has become an important export item.

ways irrigate large farming areas and are valuable sources of fish. Liberia's lagoons—such as Mesurado Lagoon and Lake Piso—run parallel to the Atlantic Ocean and are separated from the sea by narrow strips of land.

Climate

Situated in the tropics, Liberia has a moist climate, which, along with its rich, deep

A plantation worker skillfully slips a bud from a high-yielding rubber tree beneath the bark of a seedling plant.

soil, makes the land suitable for forestry and tree crops. Liberia's shoreline receives about 200 inches of rainfall a year, while its interior gets about 70 inches annually. Rain occurs primarily during the wet season, from March to October, and lets up from early July until August, a period referred to as the "middle dries." When the harmattan, a wind from the Sahara Desert, blows over Liberia in December and January, low humidity and a hazy atmosphere descend on the land.

Temperatures in Liberia range from a daytime high of 90° F in the dry season to a nighttime low of 50° F in the rainy season. February and March are the hottest, driest months, and August and September are the coolest times of the year. Because of its location, Liberia has escaped the drought problems that have struck other countries, such as Burkina Faso and Mali, farther to the north.

Photo by Mary Gemignani

Though dwindling, Liberia's rain-forests cover large areas of the country.

Independent Picture Service

The large ears of this young African elephant distinguish it from members of the Indian variety.

Flora and Fauna

Liberia's soil and varied environments support many kinds of plants and animals. The tropical rain-forests provide a high umbrella of trees, shading the cool paths below. Dracaenas, for example, are known in Europe and the United States as houseplants, but in Liberia they grow to the size of trees.

The Lagos rubber tree, which may grow to a height of 200 feet, is one of many wild plants yielding latex—the natural beginnings of rubber. The calamus palm—unable to stand by itself—sends out climbing stems hundreds of feet long, which hook on to the trunks and limbs of the tallest trees. Several species of coffee trees grow well, the best known being *Coffea liberica*. Another native plant is the kola tree, whose nuts are used for beverages and medicines. Masses of orchids, which cling to other plants but are nourished by elements in the air, carpet the forest floor or climb the tree trunks.

13

Crocodiles keep cool in Liberia's hot climate by staying close to water or by lying in mud.

The horned buffalo, or *Syncerus caffer,* is found throughout West Africa.

Independent Picture Service

Dwelling in Liberia's rivers, hippopotamuses like to spend most of their day in the water, feeding on plants and sleeping.

Sixteen species of monkeys live in Liberia, alongside elephants, buffalo, antelope, wild hogs, crocodiles, turtles, civet cats, mongooses, honey badgers, and 15 kinds of snakes. An unusual inhabitant of Liberia is the black-coated pygmy hippopotamus. This smaller member of the hippo family was first discovered in the country's rivers and was given the zoological name of *Hippopotamus liberiensis*.

Liberia's thick forests and long coastline attract flocks of birds, such as hornbills, flamingos, hawks, eagles, parrots, and woodpeckers. Perhaps the creature most commonly seen in Liberia is the bulbul, a songbird found in many parts of Africa and Asia.

Liberia has a wealth of natural environments for game animals. Nevertheless, overhunting and the gradual spread of the timber business, which often destroys animal habitats, have led to a decline in the wildlife population.

Photo by Phil Porter

Using strong but bendable liana vines, Liberians who live in the interior occasionally build intricate bridges over rivers and streams as part of a long tradition.

Monrovia

The capital city of Monrovia, established in 1824, was named for U.S. president James Monroe, who supported the relocation of freed slaves in Africa. Monrovia is the seat of government and the center of business in Liberia. In 1984 its population was 425,000. Throughout the civil conflict, refugees have poured into the capital from the countryside, swelling the city's population to as high as one million. Much of Monrovia has been damaged by fighting between military factions and will need to be rebuilt.

Independent Picture Service

Monrovia's excellent port facilities were built during World War II under an agreement with the United States. Today Liberia trades with many nations and has one of the largest merchant fleets in the world.

Courtesy of John Dean, Eliot Elisofon Archives, National Museum of African Art, Smithsonian Institution

The gridlike pattern of Monrovia's streets is evident in this aerial view of the capital.

Courtesy of Firestone Tire and Rubber Company

The center of Liberia's rubber industry, Harbel lies near the Farmington River, where some of its processing plants are located.

17

Liberia's cultural diversity is reflected on Monrovia's busy streets. Thriving ethnic communities, such as those of the Vai and the Bassa peoples, exist alongside government ministries and luxury hotels. African, U.S., and European traditions have influenced Monrovia's architecture. Churches, mosques (Islamic places of worship), and traditional African schools have been built throughout the city.

The name "Free Port of Monrovia" is posted in huge letters across the entrance to the capital's dock facilities. This now-famous port was officially opened on July 26, 1948, by the president at that time, William V. S. Tubman. Monrovia is West Africa's only free port, where freight and vessels may enter and leave without paying import duties. From its docks, ships carry goods to all parts of the world.

Secondary Cities and Important Islands

Harbel (population 60,000), about 30 miles northeast of Monrovia, owes its existence to the Firestone Tire and Rubber Company of the United States. Company workers literally carved Harbel out of the forest in 1926, when Liberia was largely rural. A separate world because of its connection to the rubber company, Harbel is Liberia's second largest city and has its own hospitals, schools, telephone system, radio station, and churches. Miles and miles of rubber trees form man-made forests—planted only since the 1920s—where thousands of people are employed to produce rubber for worldwide use.

At Buchanan (population 25,000) on the coast of central Liberia, 45,000-ton carriers are loaded with iron ore mined far inland at Mount Nimba for export to the United States, Canada, Japan, and Europe. Liberia's third largest city, Buchanan also marks the beginning of a railway line that runs along the coast to the Ivorian border.

Liberia's fourth largest urban center, Yekepa (population 16,000), owes its status to vast iron ore deposits nearby. Located in the Nimba Mountains, Yekepa is one of the few towns in the interior with both electricity and running water. Yet, as the market value of the ore drops, the city's residents leave. As a result, Yekepa is a declining community.

One of the most historic islands off Liberia's coast is Providence Island, where the first black settlers from the United States made their home. From this island the settlers explored the mainland and founded the capital city of Monrovia. Bushrod Island, now linked to Monrovia by a concrete bridge, is a busy commercial and industrial center. Nevertheless, it is most famous for being the access route to the port facilities of Monrovia.

Independent Picture Service

As a nation with a long coastline, Liberia has made good use of the small islands that are found along its shores. Factories and warehouses line the fringes of Bushrod Island, which has developed a strong industrial base through its connection with the port of Monrovia. A small tree *(center right)* stands on the edge of Providence Island, where early settlers landed in the nineteenth century.

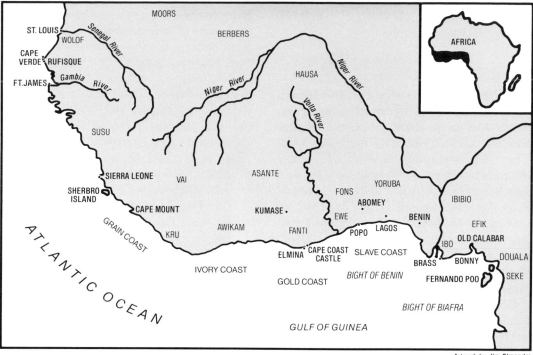

European traders gave names to the western coast of Africa in the eighteenth century. The various coastal regions—Grain Coast, Ivory Coast, Gold Coast (now Ghana)—referred to the principal commodities available in these areas. The Bights (bays) of Benin and Biafra were familiar landmarks to slave traders navigating the coast. Names of local peoples who lived in West Africa are shown on the map in light type.

2) History and Government

No written account about the area now known as Liberia predates the arrival of Europeans in the fifteenth century. Archaeological findings, however, give evidence of prehistoric settlements within the territory. Population and trade pressures in the Ghana and Mali empires, which flourished north of Liberia between the tenth and fourteenth centuries, pushed local populations southward. These peoples, in turn, pressured southern populations to move farther south. Some of these secondary immigrants ended up in what is now Liberia.

Living fairly peaceful lives as fishermen and farmers, these African groups organized over many centuries into vital communities. They developed their own forms of government and enforced their laws with strong religious ideas. Education of the young fostered community traditions. Craftspeople produced beautiful artworks, and some trading occurred, mostly among neighbors. With expanded trade contacts in the fourteenth and fifteenth centuries, however, powerful states developed at commercial crossroads in the interior of present-day Liberia. Fishermen and traders established thriving towns of up to 20,000 people along the coast.

Early Contacts

The Portuguese were the first Europeans to land on the Liberian coast. Trade pressures had sent them in search of new markets and of alternate routes to Asia. They explored much of West Africa and established Cape Palmas, at Liberia's southeastern extremity, as a navigational stop for commercial ships. Navigators named the land—including Liberia's shoreline—that lay north of the cape the Windward Coast, to distinguish it from the sheltered regions around the Gulf of Guinea to the south.

On Liberia's coast, the Kru—who had a reputation as skilled boat handlers—developed strong trade contacts with the Europeans. Acting as go-betweens in the exchange of African and European goods, Kru sailors became important because they could manage boats in the area's hazardous seas and because so few Europeans ventured inland. The Kru and others also supplied foodstuffs to passing ships. In general, however, the Africans on the Windward Coast experienced less involvement with the Europeans than did other peoples of West Africa. The landings off Liberia's coast were known to be dangerous, and better harbors existed elsewhere along the Atlantic.

In addition to European traders, Mande-speaking African groups arrived from the interior and began to push south, in some cases to avoid conflicts in their own territories. One such group, the Vai, became established on the coast near the mouth of the Mano River.

Photo by the Peabody Museum of Salem

During the years of the slave trade, Kru-speakers, who lived along the coast of Liberia, were skilled at maneuvering their boats in the rough waters of the Atlantic. Kru sailors ferried trade items and slaves from shore to the large ships that took goods and Africans to the New World.

The slaves and descendants of slaves who eventually resettled in Liberia formed part of a so-called triangle trade. Slaves were shipped from the African coast to the New World to work on the sugarcane plantations, which produced the raw materials —sugar and molasses—that were processed into rum. The rum was shipped back to West Africa where merchants organized its commercial distribution.

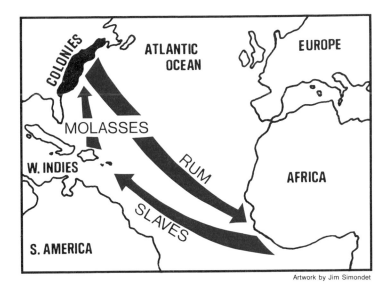

The Slave Trade

Initially, Europeans traded cloth, horses, iron implements, and copper basins for African gold, ivory, and pepper. Eventually, the capture and sale of Africans as slave laborers—mainly to work on plantations in the New World—became the most important trade activity.

Although slavery affected all of West Africa, the area that became Liberia lacked natural harbors and had difficult offshore conditions. Thus, its involvement in the slave trade was minimal compared to other areas. By the eighteenth century, most of the slave trade was concentrated in what are now Ghana, Nigeria, and Benin. Indeed, the first Americo-Liberians were descended from slaves who had been taken from these parts of West Africa.

By the end of the eighteenth century, many Europeans and North Americans argued that slavery was inhumane and should be stopped. A movement developed to provide a settlement in Africa for freed blacks who had been taken from their homes as slaves.

Cramped quarters on the slave ships and inadequate food were among the injustices inflicted on the captured Africans who made the journey to the Americas. Once they arrived, slaves could expect little more than hard work and poor living conditions.

One group, the American Colonization Society (ACS)—founded in 1816 by Robert Finley, a U.S. Presbyterian minister—was supported by humanitarian, missionary, and political organizations. Humanitarians thought slavery was barbaric, while missionaries wanted to bring the Christian religion to Africa, a place they considered to be uncivilized. Politicians from the southern United States—some of whom owned slaves—supported the idea of resettlement because they feared that successful freed or free-born blacks posed a threat to the continued existence of slavery. Indeed, the fact that slave holders were members of the ACS discouraged many blacks from participating in the resettlement scheme.

Resettlement in Africa

In 1820 the American Colonization Society sought approval from the U.S. government for their resettlement scheme. As a result, Congress granted the ACS $100,000 to help finance its plans. President James Monroe personally conveyed his support, and the *Elizabeth*—with a U.S. Navy ship as escort—was provisioned for the trip.

A native-born Virginian, James Monroe served in several political offices, both at home and abroad, before becoming president of the United States in 1817. His support of the resettlement plan of the American Colonization Society (ACS) helped to gain the scheme needed government funds.

The ship left the United States in 1820, carrying 86 emigrants. The adventurous group reached the island of Sherbro not far from the southwestern boundary of present-day Liberia, but many of these first

A nineteenth-century U.S. newspaper shows the settlement of Monrovia as it looked in the 1860s.

settlers died of regional illnesses. The island location seemed unhealthy, and the survivors moved to Sierra Leone, where a British colony of former slaves already existed.

Dr. Eli Ayres and Robert F. Stockton—the captain of the USS *Alligator*, another navy ship in the area—set out at the end of 1821 to try again to find a haven. In January 1822 the party landed at a small island in Mesurado Bay, which they named Perseverance (now Providence) Island. After negotiations with African leaders, Captain Stockton and Dr. Ayres occupied an island at the mouth of the Saint Paul River and took over a piece of land that included the area of present-day Monrovia. Stockton picked up the survivors of the earlier colonization attempt, who were waiting in nearby Sierra Leone. On April 25, 1822, all the settlers moved to the mainland.

Free-born blacks—people who were not born into slavery but who were nevertheless denied the full rights of citizenship —made up the majority of the early immigrants. Coming from the east coast of the United States, the first settlers formed independent communities under the guidance of various colonization societies, all of which were associated with the ACS. The Maryland colony, for example, was located at Cape Palmas, and a group at Bassa Cove was supported by a Pennsylvania organization. In time, the arrival of freed slaves from North America and of Africans recaptured from slave ships en route to the New World increased the settler population.

Early Settlements

The first settlers built houses and prepared the soil for crops, but heavy rains, scanty provisions, and tropical diseases caused great suffering. Moreover, African reactions to the colonists were mixed. Some leaders helped the settlers, while others—such as the Kru—resented the

Independent Picture Service

Jehudi Ashmun was one of the earliest white agents of the ACS. He helped to organize a peace treaty between some African leaders and the U.S. blacks.

Courtesy of Library of Congress

Liberia's first president, Joseph Jenkins Roberts, was originally from Virginia and governed the nation in its first years as a republic.

presence and actions of the newcomers from the United States.

Although many Africans had traded extensively with Europeans, European traders had always been merely visitors. Therefore, Africans did not view the U.S. treaties for land purchase in the same way as the settlers did; for local leaders, the new settlements were only temporary. In addition, the colonists arrived with nineteenth-century attitudes about Africa, including a feeling of superiority over the Africans and the idea that the settlers should Christianize the local populations. These biases prevented the newcomers from viewing the Africans as equals.

The first armed conflicts between the black settlers and the Africans occurred in 1822. Jehudi Ashmun, an agent of the ACS, helped to draw up a peace treaty, and the settlers and the Africans began a new but fragile coexistence. Although some groups accepted the colonists, African resistance to expansion by the Americo-Liberians continued into the twentieth century.

The ACS employed white agents to govern the black settlements for over 20 years. In 1841 Thomas Buchanan—brother of U.S. president James Buchanan—died while acting as the colony's administrator. His successor was Joseph Jenkins Roberts, formerly of Virginia—the first nonwhite to govern the colony.

The Commonwealth

Conflicts with various settlements and the ACS's financial difficulties prompted the organization to proclaim the area to be self-governing in 1841. The Pennsylvania, New York, and Mississippi communities thereafter became united under one administration—the Commonwealth of Liberia. The name Liberia, first adopted in 1824, was coined from the Latin word *liber,* which means "free." Banding together into a commonwealth also gave the colonists more self-government.

As more and more colonists arrived in Liberia, new territories were acquired by treaty with local African leaders, and set-

From 1827 to 1847, Liberia was a commonwealth. Though it had no international standing, the commonwealth's flag was patterned after the U.S. flag, with 13 stripes and a blue square in the top left-hand corner. The choice of a white cross probably is symbolic of the commonwealth's religious association with the ACS.

Artwork by Steven Woods

The flag of the Republic of Liberia is the oldest emblem continually in use on the African continent. Its design was the work of a committee of Liberian women, who chose to decrease the number of stripes from 13 to 11, since that was the number of Liberians who signed the Liberian Declaration of Independence. The white cross was replaced by a white star.

Artwork by Steven Woods

tlements sprang up all along the coast. After a few years, however, the commonwealth ran into difficulty because, as a branch of the ACS, it lacked the official status that would force foreign traders to comply with its laws. The traders refused to pay customs duties for goods or to settle fines for offenses they had committed, claiming that Liberian laws meant nothing. These foreigners did not regard Liberia as an independent nation, but rather as an experiment of U.S. humanitarians.

The Republic

Liberian port officials began to seize the ships and cargo of uncooperative traders. As a result, colonial warships, from places like Britain and France, sailed into the territorial waters of Liberia and burned settlements. The ACS, which still had authority over the area, advised the settlers to declare themselves independent. To achieve this status, Governor Roberts gave full control of the territory to the settlers.

Maryland in Africa remained outside the republic for 10 years after Liberia's independence was declared. Its flag, in use from 1834 to 1857, resembled the earlier flag of the commonwealth, to which Maryland had belonged.

Artwork by Steven Woods

25

The modernization of Monrovia has progressed quickly since this photo was taken in the early twentieth century.

In 1847 delegates from all of the colonies of the commonwealth attended a constitutional convention at Monrovia. Each representative signed the Liberian Declaration of Independence, and the convention then approved the constitution, which was closely modeled after that of the United States. The Republic of Liberia formally was announced on July 26, 1847. (Present-day Maryland county remained outside the republic, under the name Maryland in Africa until 1857.)

The Nineteenth Century

Great Britain had not shown much respect for the commonwealth, but it was the first power to recognize the new republic. France's acceptance came next, followed by the acknowledgment of other nations. The United States withheld recognition until 1862—during the presidency of Abraham Lincoln—partly because U.S. leaders believed that the southern states would not accept a black ambassador in Washington, D.C.

Liberia achieved its independence in time to provide a haven for thousands of U.S. blacks who emigrated before the Civil War of the 1860s. To provide the new arrivals with land for settlement, the Liberian government—again through treaties with local African leaders—extended the nation's boundaries. By 1860 Liberia had a 600-mile-long coastline.

The country lost much of its land, however, during the European scramble for African colonies in the 1880s. The British took over an area at the mouth of the Mano River and added it to Sierra Leone, while the French claimed the land beyond Cape Palmas for its colony, Côte d'Ivoire. Difficulties with the colonial powers were resolved by treaties—with Great Britain in 1885 and with France in 1892—that established Liberia's final borders.

Internal Tensions

Liberian society—and, consequently, its political structure—was arranged in layers during the nineteenth century. At first, the most powerful Liberians were the U.S. blacks of African-and-European ancestry, who were lighter-skinned than other blacks in the settlement. This original elite eventually ceased to exist, since few Europeans lived in the colony, and few children of mixed parentage were born. The next layer was composed of educated U.S. blacks, followed by the Africans who had been recaptured from slave ships. At the bottom of the social order were the local African groups.

Two political parties—the Republicans and the Whigs (later called the True Whigs) —emerged. The Republicans, representing the original settler elite, sought Europe's financial and technical aid to develop Liberia. The Whigs, largely made up of educated blacks, wanted to keep European influence out of Liberia and to stress Liberian nationalism. By the last quarter of the nineteenth century, the True Whig party (TWP) was in control of Liberian affairs.

Many of the original African communities within Liberian territory considered themselves independent. Consequently, they greatly resented Liberian attempts to take over their land, to tax them, and to control their trade. These ethnic groups— in particular the Kru, Gola, and Glebo— fought the government. Sometimes they enlisted the help of European—mainly British—traders, who employed Kru men on their ships. During these struggles, U.S. military assistance rescued the outnumbered Liberian settlers on several occasions.

Furthermore, economic tensions arose from the decline of coastal shipping and the reduction of prices for Liberian products. The young government was thus forced to borrow from abroad, and Liberia amassed large foreign debts.

The Twentieth Century

Financial difficulties crippled the republic during the first years of the twentieth century. European powers, concerned that Liberia's debts would not be repaid, intervened. In 1911, for example, a German

Independent Picture Service

Many of the original African groups regarded their communities as beyond the control of the government of Liberia. Here, a leader, or chief, of the Dei makes an inspection of the proposed site for a new road.

27

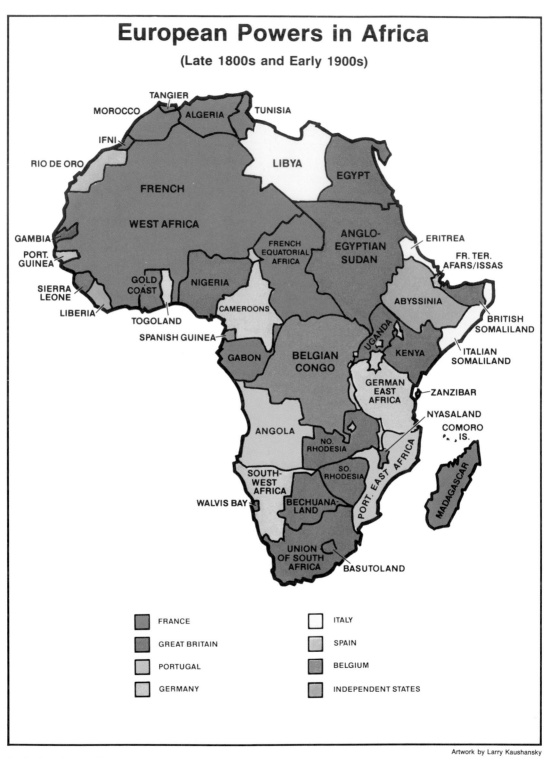

European Powers in Africa

(Late 1800s and Early 1900s)

TANGIER
MOROCCO
ALGERIA
TUNISIA
IFNI
RIO DE ORO
LIBYA
EGYPT
FRENCH
WEST AFRICA
GAMBIA
PORT. GUINEA
FRENCH EQUATORIAL AFRICA
ANGLO-EGYPTIAN SUDAN
ERITREA
FR. TER. AFARS/ISSAS
SIERRA LEONE
GOLD COAST
NIGERIA
ABYSSINIA
LIBERIA
TOGOLAND
CAMEROONS
BRITISH SOMALILAND
SPANISH GUINEA
UGANDA
KENYA
ITALIAN SOMALILAND
GABON
BELGIAN CONGO
GERMAN EAST AFRICA
ZANZIBAR
NYASALAND
COMORO IS.
ANGOLA
NO. RHODESIA
PORT. EAST AFRICA
SOUTH-WEST AFRICA
SO. RHODESIA
MADAGASCAR
WALVIS BAY
BECHUANA-LAND
UNION OF SOUTH AFRICA
BASUTOLAND

	FRANCE		ITALY
	GREAT BRITAIN		SPAIN
	PORTUGAL		BELGIUM
	GERMANY		INDEPENDENT STATES

Artwork by Larry Kaushansky

By the late nineteenth century, European powers had carved Africa into areas of influence. Liberia was the only independent republic (Abyssinia was an independent kingdom) on the entire continent. Map information taken from *The Anchor Atlas of World History*, 1978.

Firestone not only organized the planting of thousands of rubber trees but also built rows of traditional-style dwellings for the plantation workers.

gunboat entered the port of Monrovia and anchored there for a month with its guns aimed at the presidential mansion. In 1912, with the aid of the United States, Great Britain, France, and Germany, Liberia's finances were reorganized. Loans were arranged, which seemed to stabilize the nation.

World War I began in 1914, causing economic disruption in Liberia and throughout the world. The nation's income dropped to one-fourth of its prewar level. In 1915 economic depression, unemployment, and increased government repression led to a widespread revolt by Kru towns on the southern coast. Eventually, Liberia entered the global conflict on the side of the Allies and declared war on Germany in 1917. In response, the Germans sent a submarine to Monrovia, bombarded the city, and sank a ship of the Liberian navy.

For nearly a century Liberia had focused its energies on mere survival in a sometimes hostile environment. European colonial desires and Liberia's grave economic difficulties robbed the nation of political and financial stability.

The Arrival of Firestone

At this rather dismal time, the Firestone Tire and Rubber Company of Akron, Ohio, became interested in starting a vast rubber tree plantation in Liberia. Early surveys by the company in the 1920s showed that Liberia's soil and climate were suitable for the project. European efforts to control the global rubber industry by organizing colonial plantations around the world further encouraged Firestone to choose independent Liberia.

Negotiations between Firestone and the Liberian government began in 1925. Firestone was concerned about Liberia's economic instability; Liberia feared the economic domination of a large private firm over internal Liberian affairs. Several agreements were discussed, one of which proposed that Firestone should rent one million acres of land at $.06 an acre for 99 years. Another plan—insisted upon by Firestone—was a loan to Liberia of $5 million so the country could settle its debts and could assure Firestone of its economic reliability.

The rental agreement was established rather easily. The loan idea, however, caused considerable friction between the company and the Liberian people, because the loan's conditions limited Liberia's authority over its own economy. According to this second contract, Liberia could not take out any other loans. Furthermore, the loan's provisions told the Liberian government how it was to spend the money and established a U.S.-chosen—but Liberian-paid—administration to manage Liberia's financial affairs.

Although Liberians strongly objected to the loan agreement, the nation was heavily in debt and had little hope of obtaining loans from other sources. Very reluctantly, therefore, the Liberian legislature approved the agreement in 1926. In the end, Liberia got only $2.25 million of the $5 million loan.

World War II and the Tubman Era

Liberia was neutral at the beginning of World War II (1939–1945), until the government signed a mutual defense pact with the United States in 1942. The agreement allowed the United States to establish airports and military bases on Liberian soil in exchange for defending the country.

Harvey Firestone *(right),* **son of the founder of the tire company, was encouraged in his plans to find new rubber sources by Henry Ford** *(left)* **and Thomas Edison** *(center).*

Flanked by bodyguards and aides, Liberian president William V. S. Tubman enters his official limousine.

In 1959 President Tubman *(center left)* and his vice president William Tolbert *(left)* met with officials of the government of newly independent Ghana, including its president, Kwame Nkrumah *(center right).*

In 1944 Liberia declared war on Germany, hoping that an alliance with the victors might bring later economic rewards from the United States.

After World War II, Liberia developed an open policy to encourage foreign economic investment. Although this influx of money led to growth in the Liberian economy, most of the profits left the country. Money that remained in Liberia enriched only the Americo-Liberian elite. Many Liberians continued to suffer from poverty and poor social conditions. The economic upturn, however, allowed Liberia to pay off the Firestone loan in 1952—a cause for great national celebration.

Although the light-skinned elite had disappeared from politics in the nineteenth century, a definite ruling class still existed. From the last years of World War II until 1971, William V. S. Tubman dominated Liberian politics. He was a member of the True Whig party, which had won every presidential election since 1878. This group controlled national affairs but left much of the local administration and tax collection in the hands of local leaders, or chiefs.

Tubman, however, and his successor, William R. Tolbert, encouraged the African majority to become more active in the political system. But neither leader had any intention of letting go of the TWP's powerful position in Liberian national affairs. Thus, the Africans—who generally had few economic or political opportunities—could advance only by becoming part of the elite and by rejecting ties to their own families and communities.

Even if Africans wanted to participate in national affairs, the True Whig party carefully controlled the flow of funds, jobs, and power, thus reducing the impact of African participation. Only in the lower

31

ranks of the military were Africans able to establish a strong presence. Indeed, until voting restrictions were eased somewhat in the middle of the twentieth century, only landowners could vote. Moreover, there was usually only one candidate—from the TWP—for each office.

The 1980 Military Coup and Its Aftermath

An economic recession in the 1970s hit low-income Liberians the hardest. In 1979 President Tolbert announced a huge increase in the price of rice in order to encourage greater production. Critics of the government increased their political activities, forming opposition parties, such as the Progressive People's party (PPP), to challenge those in power. Protests developed, and Liberian police forces killed nearly 140 demonstrators. The PPP called a general strike to stop activity in all services and industries in March 1980, after which the PPP party leaders were arrested on charges of treason.

A military coup d'état led by Master Sergeant Samuel K. Doe, from rural Grand Gedeh county, prevented the trials from taking place. The soldiers killed President Tolbert and key members of his cabinet, and the power of the TWP and the Americo-Liberian elite was broken. Although some Liberians left the country, in general the coup was widely supported within the nation.

After the coup, Doe's People's Redemption Council (PRC) eliminated—sometimes by execution—TWP leaders from Liberian politics. The military government promised elections and new freedoms, and the assortment of people in power changed dramatically. Nevertheless, as in the past, the press was restricted, and the only political parties that could operate were those approved by the government.

Doe assumed the presidency in 1985, after an election that most observers felt

Tubman's successor, William R. Tolbert, relaxed press restrictions slightly during his tenure as president. Here, he is being interviewed while traveling on an airplane.

Courtesy of Elwood Dunn

In April 1979 riots erupted near the executive mansion in Monrovia over the president's decision to raise the price of rice. Liberian police killed many civilians during the riots.

Courtesy of Elwood Dunn

Samuel K. Doe led the military coup d'état in 1980 that resulted in the deaths of several members of the Tolbert government, including the president. Doe is the first Liberian head of state who is from an African ethnic group.

was dishonest. Doe's opponents made several unsuccessful attempts to overthrow his government. Near the end of 1989, a former government official, Charles Taylor, led an opposition group called the National Patriotic Front of Liberia (NPFL) in the first battle of Liberia's long and bloody civil war. Months later Taylor entered Monrovia and proclaimed himself the president of an interim (temporary) government. In September 1990, the NPFL captured and executed Doe.

Taylor's claim to power was soon challenged—first by dissenters within the NPFL, and then by other militant groups that had sprung up in the NPFL's wake. In the meantime, Liberia's neighboring countries sent a peacekeeping force to try to restore order. The peacekeeping effort has been largely ineffective. Some foreign troops have even committed looting and human rights offenses—abuses the soldiers were sent to control.

In 1981 local support for the new regime – called the People's Redemption Council (PRC) – was strong.

Though some African leaders were concerned about the political violence that erupted in Liberia after the coup, others showed their support. The president of Guinea, Sékou Touré, met with Samuel K. Doe in 1980.

In the years following the NPFL's initial attack, many attempts have been made to stop the fighting and to hold elections. Each time a ceasefire is declared, one militia or another breaks the peace. Liberia has made some progress toward installing an interim government, but the process is often slowed or interrupted by the warlords's refusals to participate in a political solution to the conflict.

In September 1995, a temporary Council of State was sworn in and a politically neutral president, William Sankawulo, was chosen. A year later, Ruth Perry replaced Sankawulo as president and became Africa's first female head of state. The council and president are to stay in power until free elections are held.

It is estimated that 150,000 Liberians were killed in the civil war between 1989 and 1995. About 750,000 fled the country as refugees, and an additional 1.2 million left their homes but remain in Liberia.

Government

The Liberian Constitution of 1986 calls for a government similar in many ways to those described in previous Liberian constitutions—with a presidential system, a bicameral (two-house) legislature, and an independent judiciary. The document establishes the president as head of state (a ceremonial role), head of the government (a political post), and commander in chief of the armed forces. The legislature consists of a house of representatives and a senate, which together make Liberia's laws. The judicial branch enforces the laws through its court system, of which the supreme court is the highest judicial body.

A series of interim governments has been formed and dissolved since the beginning of Liberia's civil war, but none has yet succeeded in arranging elections. Meanwhile, military leaders challenge the authority of the nation's constitution and dispute the basic form of government.

Liberia's two-house legislature meets in a modern structure located on Capitol Hill in Monrovia.

Three young Kpelle children play in the sand outside their house in the village of Mobuta, located in west central Liberia.

3) The People

Liberia has approximately 2.1 million people. About 5 percent are Americo-Liberians, and the rest belong to 16 major ethnic groups, each with its own language. English is the official tongue and is taught in the schools, but two of the coastal groups, the Vai and the Glebo, also read and write in their own language.

African Groups

The Kru, Bassa, Glebo, Dei, and Vai live along the coast. In the northern and west-ern areas of the nation are the homes of the Kissi, Bandi, Malinke, Kuwaa, Mende, Gola, and Loma. The Kpelle live in the central region. The Gio, Mano, and Krahn inhabit eastern areas of Liberia. The largest groups are the Kpelle and the Bassa. People of all areas, especially women, are active in farming.

An important way to distinguish these groups from one another is according to the main language they speak. Three Niger-Congo language clusters—Kru, Mande, and West Atlantic—exist in Liberia.

Most crops in Liberia are grown for the family to eat. When there is a surplus, women bring the produce to local markets to sell. This woman carries a bucket of mangoes to Salala, the market town nearest to her village.

Photo by Sally Humphrey

Photo by Mary Gemignani

A Gola elder is carried through his village by his followers as part of a traditional ceremony.

Kru-speakers include the Bassa, Krahn, and Kuwaa peoples. Among the Mande-speakers are the Vai, Kpelle, Mano, Malinke, Gio, Loma, Mende, and Bandi. The Gola and the Kissi are the main speakers of the West Atlantic tongues. There are also many subdivisions of these major language groups. Most Liberians are multilingual, often speaking two and sometimes as many as four languages fluently.

Most ethnic groups in the west, northwest, and central regions participate in traditional secret societies—the Poro (for men) and the Sande (for women). These groups teach young people the traditions of their ethnic group and prepare them for their roles in the community. In all Liberian ethnic groups, elders traditionally hold power.

Some ethnic communities are noted for a particular religion, craft, or profession. For example, the Vai are mostly Muslim (followers of Islam), and the Malinke, who are also Muslim, are famous traders. The Kru and Glebo are skilled fishermen and boat handlers.

Courtesy of Agency for International Development

Although many Liberians still live in rural areas, urban dwellers—especially in Monrovia—have access to training in the latest technologies.

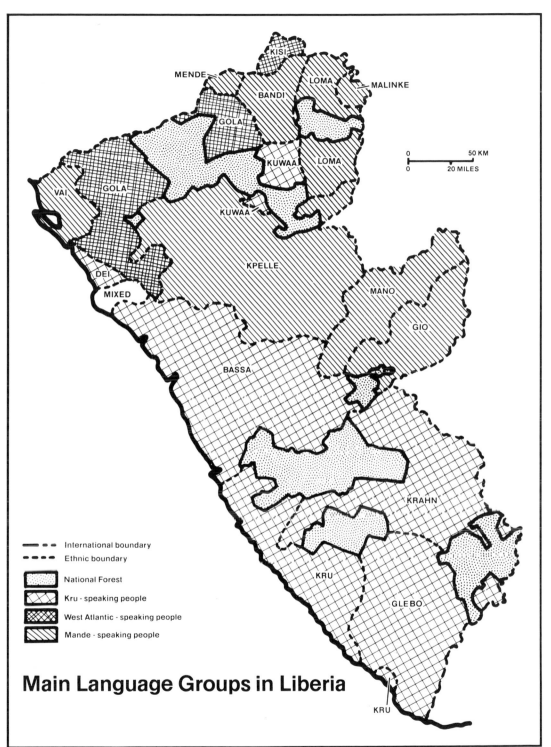

Main Language Groups in Liberia

Liberia's language groups fall into three main clusters. Kru-speakers live mostly along the coast and in east central sections of the country. People who use West Atlantic languages tend to reside in western Liberia. Mande-speakers generally dwell in north and northwestern regions.

A young Liberian mother, surrounded by her four children, holds the child of a U.S. missionary who works in Liberia.

The Americo-Liberians

The Americo-Liberian group is slowly adjusting to its new, less-influential position in Liberian politics and society. These descendants of American colonists have traditionally controlled Liberia's government and most of its wealth.

People from African ethnic groups had long resented the imbalance of power. This resentment came to a head in 1980 with the military coup of Master Sergeant Samuel K. Doe, a member of the Krahn ethnic group, against the Americo-Liberian-controlled government. Following the coup, power struggles have been played out along ethnic lines, largely between members of the Krahn, Mandingo, Mano, and Gio peoples. Some Liberians have accused military leader Charles Taylor, who is part Americo-Liberian, of attempting to restore the old political order.

Religion

Religion has always been a powerful force in Liberian life. Within traditional African societies, religious beliefs, political structures, and social behavior are closely linked.

The majority of Liberians hold traditional African beliefs, and 20 percent are Muslim. Conversion to Christianity is widespread, however, and the main Christian sects are the Methodists, Baptists, Presbyterians, Episcopalians, Lutherans, Roman Catholics, and Seventh Day Adventists. The Baptists were the earliest to arrive when Lott Carey, a black minister, founded Liberia's first church in 1822.

Education

Liberia has a long history of both traditional African and European-style education. In the traditional schools of the Poro and Sande societies, boys and girls learn adult skills such as hunting, farming, medical and healing techniques, music and dance, and correct social behavior. In the past, children entered these schools for four to seven years and were considered adults when they emerged. Many young people attend these traditional institutions, called bush schools, during their vacation from European-style educational facilities.

During the Tubman administration in the 1950s and 1960s, many elementary schools were constructed throughout the country. In the 1970s the government expanded the number of secondary schools. Due to lack of national funds, many schools are privately run, and most of these are financed by Christian churches. About 40 percent of the population is literate, and about half of Liberia's school-aged children attend elementary classes. Secondary schools enroll about 20 percent of the qualified population. At times, poor economic conditions and political instability have severely hampered the educational system, and unpaid teachers have had

Courtesy of S. M. A. Fathers

Most Christian church officials try to work within the existing structure of African communities, sometimes by meeting with the elders of the village.

Photo by Sally Humphrey

Children line up to enter their government-run local school. Missionaries and international businesses also operate or support schools in Liberia.

Young girls from western regions of Liberia participate in the traditional ceremonies of the Sande society, after which they will be considered adults within their communities.

Cuttington University College is supported by the Liberian government and several Christian churches.

Village schools, though often crowded and understaffed, have helped to increase the number of Liberians who can read and write.

to strike for their wages, or to look for other employment.

Except for a yearly registration fee, primary and secondary education are provided to children at no cost to their families. Students who continue their education at the university level pay only half their tuition, and the government pays the other half.

Liberia College opened in 1863 and has since been renamed the University of Liberia (LU). Located in Monrovia, the campus has facilities to train young Liberians in the liberal arts, science, education, law, medicine, and other professions. About 3,000 students attended the university in 1988. Financial setbacks have affected LU throughout the Doe regime and the civil war. Students have also reacted to their nation's political turmoil, demonstrating against the government or in support of teachers' strikes.

In Liberia's interior is Cuttington University College (founded in 1889), which serves a smaller student body. A Christian institution, Cuttington is owned by the Episcopal Church and is supported financially by the government.

Many schools like this one were closed during Liberia's civil war. Instead of receiving an education, many children were conscripted as soldiers.

Independent Picture Service

43

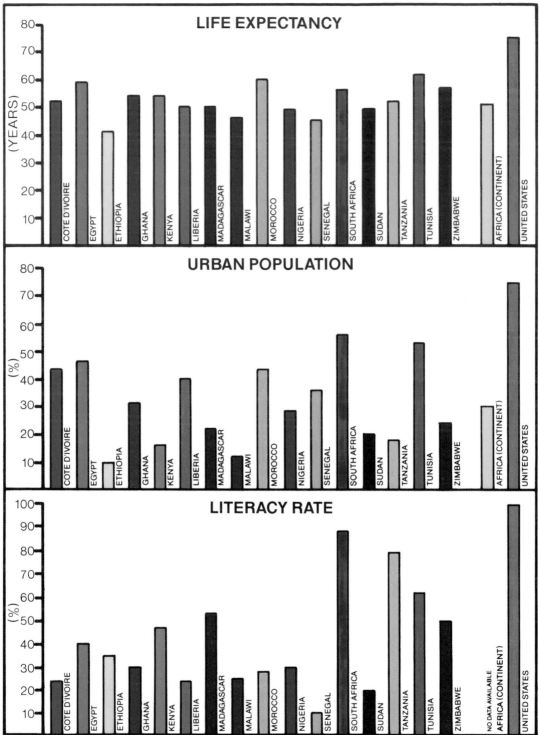

LIFE EXPECTANCY

(YEARS)

COTE D'IVOIRE · EGYPT · ETHIOPIA · GHANA · KENYA · LIBERIA · MADAGASCAR · MALAWI · MOROCCO · NIGERIA · SENEGAL · SOUTH AFRICA · SUDAN · TANZANIA · TUNISIA · ZIMBABWE · AFRICA (CONTINENT) · UNITED STATES

URBAN POPULATION

(%)

COTE D'IVOIRE · EGYPT · ETHIOPIA · GHANA · KENYA · LIBERIA · MADAGASCAR · MALAWI · MOROCCO · NIGERIA · SENEGAL · SOUTH AFRICA · SUDAN · TANZANIA · TUNISIA · ZIMBABWE · AFRICA (CONTINENT) · UNITED STATES

LITERACY RATE

(%)

COTE D'IVOIRE · EGYPT · ETHIOPIA · GHANA · KENYA · LIBERIA · MADAGASCAR · MALAWI · MOROCCO · NIGERIA · SENEGAL · SOUTH AFRICA · SUDAN · TANZANIA · TUNISIA · ZIMBABWE · NO DATA AVAILABLE AFRICA (CONTINENT) · UNITED STATES

Artwork by Jim Simondet

The three factors depicted in this graph suggest differences in the quality of life among 16 African nations. Averages for the United States and the entire continent of Africa are included for comparison. Data taken from "1987 World Population Data Sheet" and *PC-Globe.*

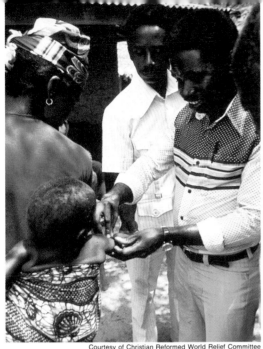

Courtesy of Christian Reformed World Relief Committee

A local medical practitioner checks the health of a Liberian baby, who is still strapped to its mother's back.

Courtesy of S. M. A. Fathers

Surrounded by her anxious children, a Liberian mother waits her turn at a health clinic in Grand Cess, a town on Liberia's southeastern coast.

Health

In Liberia the extended family takes responsibility for the young, the aged, the ill, and the disabled. Those who live in cities—where most hospitals are located—benefit from the best medical facilities. Villagers must depend on small government clinics and traditional healers for

Courtesy of Christian Reformed World Relief Committee

Villagers examine a newly built well, which will safeguard them from the diseases caused by impure water.

Once they begin teaching their own classes, these physical education trainees will be able to show young Liberians the importance of keeping fit.

their medical care. During the 1960s and 1970s, the government built many maternity and outpatient clinics in the countryside. The declining economy of the 1980s, however, slowed the opening of new clinics and reduced the quality and availability of existing health care.

In 1996 life expectancy in Liberia was 58 years of age. Although this is average for Africa as a whole, it is well below European or North American levels. Better maternity and child health care, as well as immunization programs to combat yaws (a skin disease), tuberculosis, and malaria, have lowered the nation's infant mortality rate. Liberia loses 113 babies out of every 1,000 born in the country, a rate that exceeds Africa's average of 91 per 1,000. Another area of health concern is the availability of safe drinking water. Impure water has been responsible for cholera outbreaks, especially in heavily populated areas.

Improved child health care—including local clinics that instruct mothers about hygiene—has lowered Liberia's infant mortality rate.

Communications

Newspapers have been a part of Liberian society throughout its history. The nation's first news publication, the *Liberia Herald*, began circulating in 1826. During the Tubman era, the government discouraged complaints in the press. Tolbert's administration encouraged some openness, but the Doe regime and subsequent interim governments have maintained restrictions on the press. Government officials have sometimes put reporters or editors in prison or shut down their operations. Many journalists elect to censor their own writings in favor of the government or powerful military groups. Others have openly criticized Liberian leaders, and some reporters have faced threats or even beatings for their stories. But the government has sometimes backed down from its demands for censor-

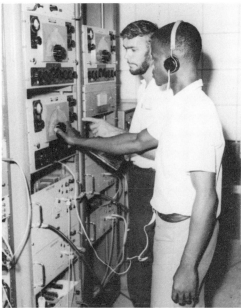

Independent Picture Service

A student receives on-the-job training at station **ELTV** in Monrovia.

Courtesy of Voice of America

Voice of America (VOA) is the broadcasting service of the United States Information Agency, whose aim is to explain the policies of the United States to the citizens of other countries. The VOA, whose only African station *(above)* is in Liberia, airs educational and cultural programs in many languages throughout the world.

Red nuts that grow on oil palm trees are plentiful in Liberia and are the beginnings of palm butter soup, a meal often eaten with rice.

ship after journalists banded together to complain.

Television continues to have great impact, and the national station, ELTV, broadcasts every night. Half a dozen radio stations, as well as the Voice of America (the only VOA station in Africa), relay information within Liberia. Many radio programs have been subjected to government censorship.

Cultural Traditions

Dancing, drama, and music are among the cultural activities enjoyed by the people of Liberia. Every farm community has its own drummers and other musicians, who

Weaving is a traditional craft throughout Liberia. This man produces long strips of cloth that will be sewn together to make blankets, shirts, or full-length robes.

48

provide entertainment for festivals, weddings, and school graduations. Professional dance troupes sometimes arrive in towns and villages for special celebrations.

Painting is highly developed in the coastal areas, where dyes obtained from roots, leaves, and tree bark are used to decorate homes and masks. Craftspeople such as ivory-workers, wood-carvers, weavers, goldsmiths, and leather workers produce jewelry, cloth, and a variety of musical instruments.

In both rural and urban areas, Liberia's African traditions continue with vitality. The importance of the family unit is strong and includes not only immediate relatives but everyone in the community. Urban lifestyles and European-style education have not diminished the sense of community responsibility toward raising children and caring for older people.

Food

Traditionally in Liberian households, rice is eaten twice a day. Other starches are cassavas (fleshy roots), sweet potatoes, eddoes (another edible root), plantains (bananalike fruits), and sweet corn. *Fufu*—a sticky dough—is often made from cassavas or plantains and is generally served with spicy sauces made with palm oil, greens, or tomatoes. Pepper soup seasoned with bits of meat or fish sometimes completes the typical meal.

Fresh fruits and vegetables abound in Liberia. Oranges, grapefruits, avocados, bananas, pineapples, and watermelons are grown commercially and in family gardens. Cucumbers, okra, collards, eggplants, and lima beans are widely cultivated and sold in markets, and salad greens—a special Liberian favorite—are also readily available.

Courtesy of Christian Reformed World Relief Committee

Surrounded by examples of his work, a Liberian wood-carver explains his technique.

Using long, wide knives called cutlasses, a group of young Liberians clears the grass from a field. After the vegetation has been cut down, the dead plants are burned, and the field is ready for sowing.

4) The Economy

Liberia's civil war is ruining the country's economy. Most commercial activity has ceased or is operated illicitly. Foreign investors have pulled out of the country, and production facilities are damaged or destroyed. Unemployment has skyrocketed, approaching 90 percent.

The nation has considerable potential for wealth, however, and could rebuild and prosper under a stable government. Liberia could then resume its position as an exporter of iron ore, rubber, timber, cacao (from which chocolate is made), coffee, palm kernels and oil, and diamonds.

Agriculture

The majority of Liberians are farmers. Traditional farming methods are well adapted to soil, climate, and labor conditions. Agricultural development projects must be carefully suited to local conditions, since Western farming techniques may not be appropriate. In rural areas,

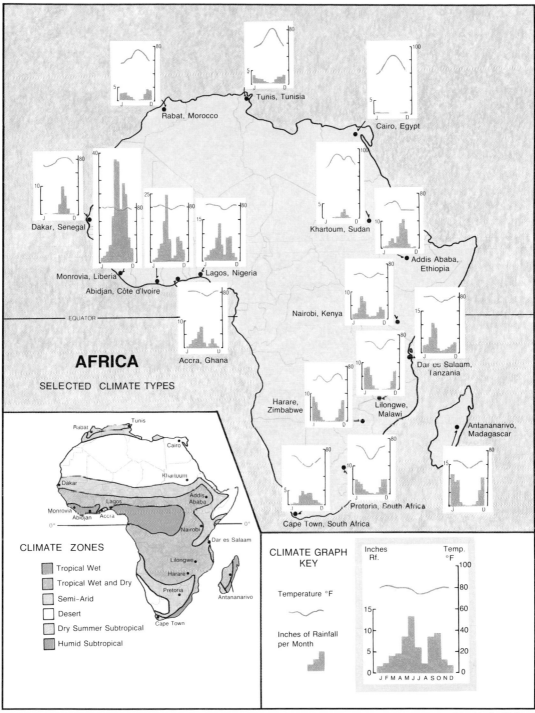

AFRICA

SELECTED CLIMATE TYPES

Rabat, Morocco

Tunis, Tunisia

Cairo, Egypt

Dakar, Senegal

Khartoum, Sudan

Monrovia, Liberia

Abidjan, Côte d'Ivoire

Lagos, Nigeria

Addis Ababa, Ethiopia

EQUATOR

Accra, Ghana

Nairobi, Kenya

Dar es Salaam, Tanzania

Harare, Zimbabwe

Lilongwe, Malawi

Antananarivo, Madagascar

Pretoria, South Africa

Cape Town, South Africa

CLIMATE ZONES

- Tropical Wet
- Tropical Wet and Dry
- Semi–Arid
- Desert
- Dry Summer Subtropical
- Humid Subtropical

Rabat
Tunis
Cairo
Khartoum
Dakar
Addis Ababa
Lagos
Monrovia
Abidjan
Accra
0°
Nairobi
Dar es Salaam
Lilongwe
Harare
Pretoria
Antananarivo
Cape Town

CLIMATE GRAPH KEY

Inches Rf.

Temp. °F

Temperature °F

Inches of Rainfall per Month

J F M A M J J A S O N D

Artwork by Carol F. Barrett

These climate graphs show the monthly change in the average rainfall received and in the average temperature from January to December for the capital cities of 16 African nations. On the graph for Monrovia, Liberia, note that January and February are dry, especially in comparison to the very wet months of June and July. Data taken from *World-Climates* by Willy Rudloff, Stuttgart, 1981.

Freshly picked rice dries in the sun. Women are very active in the agricultural sector of Liberia's economy, growing most of the family's food.

A worker pours rice—Liberia's staple food crop—into a sack at the Central Experiment Station in Suakoko. From here, the rice will be shipped to regional and national vendors.

These farmers work together to plant an entire field in neat rows.

Independent Picture Service

where most Liberians have traditionally lived, families supply much of their own food by growing rice, fruits, and vegetables. Many Liberians also grow cash crops (produce for sale), such as coffee and cacao, and often sell their surplus rice through cooperatives to local merchants or national marketing boards. Women are the main farmers of food for the family, while men usually grow the cash crops.

In the 1970s, the government, with assistance from international agencies, financed large agricultural projects to cultivate tree crops—such as citrus fruits and cacao—as well as rice and sugarcane, for commercial purposes. Some of these ideas were successful, while others failed because of a lack of laborers, problems with farm machinery, and breakdowns in marketing and transportation.

Courtesy of Agency for International Development

Coffee beans are packed into sacks before further processing and shipment to international markets.

Courtesy of S. M. A. Fathers

Within sight of her village, a farmer hoes the communal garden.

Photo by Phil Porter

Rubber trees grow well in Liberia's tropical climate, thriving on large plantations set up by the Firestone Tire and Rubber Company in the 1920s.

Courtesy of S. M. A. Fathers

Bearing the scars of previous tappings, a grove of rubber trees continues to be worked by a Liberian plantation employee.

After a downward, circular cut has been made in the bark of the rubber tree, the latex, or milky white fluid, collects in a small pan. Each tapping—the name for the bark-cutting process—yields about one fluid ounce of latex.

The Rubber Industry

Rubber tree cultivation and processing requires a huge labor force, and the industry has been the largest employer in the nation. Liberia is one of the world's biggest rubber producers. In the 1980s rubber accounted for 16 percent of exports.

The Firestone Tire and Rubber Company began its plantations in Liberia in the 1920s, but the Great Depression of the 1930s limited its operations. During World War II, however, when Japan occupied the major rubber-producing countries in eastern Asia, Liberia emerged as a valuable source of rubber for the Allied war effort. Planting continued in the postwar years, with the B.F. Goodrich and Uniroyal companies following Firestone's lead in estab-

lishing plantations in Liberia. (Goodrich later sold its holdings to a British firm.) Rubber was Liberia's largest source of revenue until 1961, when income from iron ore mining outpaced rubber for the first time.

Firestone suspended operations in 1992 because of concerns for wartime safety. Before the company's shutdown, its two plantations at Harbel and Cavalla cultivated 10 million trees on 90,000 acres and employed a few thousand Liberians. In the 1980s Firestone provided about 51 percent of Liberia's rubber output. Other foreign companies accounted for 13 percent, and independent farmers produced the remaining 36 percent.

A driver monitors his truck's pumps as they force collected latex into troughs for a quality and purity check.

Acid is added to the collected latex to make it coagulate, or become solid and rubbery. The material is then pressed between rollers into sheets.

Workers wind rubberized latex around large drums to simplify the process of cutting it into sheets.

The sheets of rubber are hung to dry in a special room at the processing factory. When thoroughly dried, the sheets will be shipped to another plant for further refinement into rubber products.

The Bong Mining Company operates its complex in central Liberia.

Mining

The mining of iron ore has provided the largest part of Liberia's export earnings. The nation's rich deposits of iron ore were discovered in the 1940s. The Nimba range holds over 200 million tons, and regions near the Bomi Hills, the Bassa Hills, the Putu range, and the Mano River all contain huge reserves.

Two major companies—the Bong Mining Company and the National Iron Ore Company—have run iron-mining operations in Liberia. Until recently, the Liberian-Swedish American Mining Company (LAMCO) was also a participant. Its role in Liberia's mining sector is being phased out. Iron ore production began in 1953, when the Liberian government gave the International African-American Corporation (IAAC) the

Iron ore moves by conveyer belt to a waiting cargo ship at Monrovia's docks.

right to mine 500 square miles in north-eastern Liberia. Explorations uncovered the vast wealth of Nimba, and steel companies from all corners of the world began asking to participate.

The IAAC, however, was too small to handle this flood of requests, and a complex financial structure—known as the LAMCO Joint-Venture Enterprise—was set up in 1960. This joint venture has invested heavily in a 175-mile railway and in a deepwater port at Buchanan to accommodate 45,000-ton ore ships.

Diamonds, discovered in 1957, caused a diamond rush of giant proportions as workers from all parts of Liberia gave up their jobs to try to get rich quickly. Since then, diamond mining has been carefully controlled by the government, although Malinke traders often arrive in Monrovia with stones of enormous value.

Large iron ore deposits in the Nimba Mountains brought many developers to the region.

With its acres of wooded land, Liberia has developed timber into its third largest export.

On the beaches of Grand Cess, a Liberian fisherman displays his net, which he uses to collect the variety of seafood living in the coastal waters.

Because of overcutting for both fuel and timber products, Liberia's rain-forests are shrinking.

Forestry and Fishing

Liberia's rain-forests—which cover more than 80 percent of the land area and which contain more than 250 species of trees—are among the largest timber reserves on the African continent. The government administers 8.7 million acres of trees. Teak, mahogany, and African walnut are the most commercially valuable woods and are used in furniture making, heavy construction, and general carpentry. Earnings from timber exports doubled from 1977 to 1979. Although a decline occurred in the 1980s and although Liberia's rain-forests are shrinking rapidly, timber is still Liberia's third largest export item.

Despite its 350-mile-long Atlantic coast, Liberia has yet to develop fishing into a major industry. In the last decade, however, commercial deepwater fishing has increased, and typical catches include lobster, crab, shrimp, and sole. Within the country, over 600 specialized fish farms are in operation.

59

Road building was a major item on Liberia's public works agenda throughout the 1980s.

Transportation and Shipping

Liberia's network of roads includes both government-constructed projects and privately owned roads open to public use. The country's main highway is the Monrovia-Sanniquellie Road. From Monrovia the highway leads northeastward to the Guinea border near Ganta and eastward to Liberia's boundary with Côte d'Ivoire. Other roads connect Monrovia with Buchanan and Freetown, the capital of Sierra Leone. Liberia's road system is linked to that of Sierra Leone by a bridge over the Mano River.

Technicians monitor the incoming and outgoing flights at Robertsfield International Airport.

In Monrovia, cars and buses are the main forms of transport. Buses also provide service to the Liberian interior.

Two airports serve the air travel needs of Liberia. The Spriggs Payne Airfield, located in a suburb of Monrovia, handles domestic flights of Air Liberia, the national airline formed during the Tolbert administration. International travel facilities are provided by Roberts International Airport, situated about 40 miles from the capital. There are more than 100 major airstrips scattered throughout the country.

Liberia has the world's second largest merchant fleet. Shipowners are encouraged to register their vessels in Liberia because the government imposes low taxes and because duty-free port facilities exist in Monrovia. Although they fly the Liberian flag, few of these ships dock in Liberian ports. The National Port Authority controls most of the country's harbors.

Until recently, towns along Liberia's southeastern coast had no road access to the main highways. Here, workers clear the land to make a 60-mile feeder road.

The Future

Before Liberia's civil war, the nation's prosperity depended greatly on the sale of its raw materials to world markets. The income that these products generated went to the government and to wealthy Liberians. Most of the Liberian people remained poor.

Liberia's economy fluctuated according to world demand for its few exports. In the 1980s, economic downturns in the United States and Europe led to a decline in Liberia's earnings. With the wartime halt of most business activities, Liberia's main income comes from revenues from its large registry of foreign ships.

If the nation's key military and political players can move toward building a stable government, Liberia may once again focus on its long-term goals. The country must control its debt and manage the serious health, education, and housing needs of its

Many ships use Monrovia's duty-free port facilities to unload their cargo, and Liberian-registered vessels carry goods throughout the world.

Between villages, it is sometimes easier to travel by dugout canoe than overland.

A Kpelle woman uses a local stream as her water supply, which she needs for both cooking and drinking water.

growing population. Liberia's challenge will be to develop its human and natural resources to restore an economic base and to improve the lives of all its citizens.

The sale of surplus home-produced goods often takes place at local markets.

Index